THE PRAYERS

Sarah Blue

I LOVE

SELECTED AND EDITED BY
DAVID A REDDING

CALLIGRAPHY BY
ALICE GIRAND

ILLUSTRATED BY
SARAH BLUE

Strawberry Hill Press

Strawberry Hill Press
616 44th Avenue
San Francisco, CA, 94121

Distributed by Stackpole Books
Cameron and Kelker Sts.
Harrisburg, PA, 17105

Book Edited by A. Jean Lesher
Book Design by Alice Girand
Manufactured in the United States of America

Library of Congress Cataloging in Publication Data
Main entry under title:

The Prayers I Love.

        Bibliography: p.
        1. Prayers. I. Redding, David A II. Girand, Alice, 1938-
BV245. P853   242'.8   78-17798
ISBN 0-89407-025-8

dedicated to

velma pierce

whom we love

By

Thy help

this shall

come fresh

from the heart

Permit it also to go to the heart

Sören Kierkegaard
1813-1855

Lord, make me an
instrument of Thy peace

where there is hatred let me sow
Love

where there is injury pardon

where there is doubt faith

where there is despair hope

where there is darkness light

and
where
there is
sadness joy

O Divine Master

                grant that
I may not so much seek
to be consoled as

                    to console

to be undersood as

                    to understand

to be loved as to love

                        for it is in giving
                        that we receive
                        it is in pardoning
                    that we are pardoned
and
    it is in dying that we are
        born to eternal life

                st. francis of assisi
                    1182 - 1226

LORD
THOU KNOWEST
I SHALL BE VERIE BUSIE
THIS DAY

I MAY FORGET THEE

DO NOT THOU
FORGET ME

BARON JACOB ASTLEY
BEFORE THE BATTLE OF EDGEHILL
OCTOBER 1642

Thou hast
made us for
Thyself
                and
        our hearts
are restless until
they rest in Thee

st. augustine
AD 354-430

O Thou full of compassion
I commit & commend myself unto Thee
    in Whom I am & live & know
Be Thou the goal of my pilgrimmage
    and my rest by the way
Let me take refuge from the crowding
    turmoil of wordly thoughts
        beneath the shadow of Thy wings
And let my heart
        this sea of restlessness
        find peace in Thee, O God

adapted from St. Augustine

I LOOKED
FOR MY SOUL
BUT MY SOUL
I COULD
NOT SEE

I LOOKED
FOR MY GOD
BUT MY GOD
ELUDED ME

I LOOKED
FOR A FRIEND
AND THEN I
FOUND ALL THREE

THOMAS BLAKE
ATTRIBUTION

GOD GRANT ME

THE SERENITY TO ACCEPT
THE THINGS I CANNOT CHANGE

THE COURAGE TO CHANGE
THE THINGS I CAN

AND THE

WISDOM
TO KNOW THE
DIFFERENCE

AUTHOR UNKNOWN

O GOD, BLESS
ALL THE MEN HERE WITH LONG HAIR
AND ALL THOSE WITH SHORT HAIR
AND ALL THOSE WITH NO HAIR AND HELP

THEM TO LOVE EACH OTHER

FOR CHRIST'S SAKE

AMEN

BOOGER BOLES

O Thou unknown
Almighty Cause of all my hope and fear!
In whose dread Presence, ere an hour,
perhaps I must appear!

If I have wander'd in
those paths of life I ought to shun
As something loudly in my breast
remonstrates I have done

Thou know'st that
Thou hast formed me with passions wild and strong
And listning to their witching voice
has often led me wrong

Where human weakness
has come short or frailty stept aside
Do Thou, All Good, for such Thou art,
in shades of darkness hide

Where with intention I have err'd
no other plea I have
But THOU ART GOOD
and Goodness
still delighteth
to forgive—

Robert Burns
1759-1796

NOW I LAY ME DOWN TO SLEEP

I PRAY THE LORD MY SOUL TO KEEP

IF I SHOULD DIE BEFORE I WAKE

I PRAY THE LORD MY SOUL TO TAKE

AMEN

A CHILD'S PRAYER

Depart now in the
fellowship of God the Father
and as you go, Remember —

in the Goodness of
    God you were born into this world

by the Grace of
    God you have been kept
     all the day long
        Even until this hour

and by the Love of God
    fully revealed in the face of Jesus

    You are being Redeemed

The Rev. Dr. John R. Claypool
1971

Lead me
Lord
Lead me in
Thy righteousness

make Thy way plain
before my face

for it is Thou
Lord
Thou O Lord
only
Who makest me
dwell in safety

The Concord Anthem Book

I asked God for strength
       that I might achieve
I was made weak
    that I might learn to obey

I asked for health
  that I might do greater things
I was given infirmity
    that I might do better things

I asked for riches
         that I might be happy
I was given poverty
         that I might be wise

I asked for power
         that I might have the praise of men
I was given weakness
         that I might feel the need of God

I asked for all things
      that I might enjoy LIFE that I might enjoy
               all things

I received
nothing that
I asked for
but all that I
had hoped for....

My
prayers
were answered....

Prayer of an Unknown
Confederate Soldier

OH LORD
I'VE NEVER LIVED WHERE CHURCHES GROW
I LOVE CREATION BETTER AS IT STOOD THAT DAY YOU
FINISHED IT SO LONG AGO AND LOOKED UPON
YOUR WORK AND CALLED IT GOOD
I KNOW THAT OTHERS FIND YOU IN THE LIGHT THAT'S SIFTED
DOWN THROUGH TINTED WINDOW PANES
AND YET I SEEM TO FEEL YOU NEAR TONIGHT IN THIS DIM
QUIET STARLIGHT ON THE PLAINS

I THANK YOU LORD
THAT I AM PLACED SO WELL
THAT YOU HAVE MADE MY FREEDOM SO COMPLETE
THAT I'M NO SLAVE OF WHISTLE, CLOCK OR BELL
NOR WEAK-EYED PRISONER OF WALL AND STREET

JUST LET ME LIVE MY LIFE AS I'VE BEGUN AND
GIVE ME WORK THAT'S OPEN TO THE SKY
MAKE ME A PARDNER OF THE WIND AND SUN
AND I WON'T ASK A LIFE THAT'S SOFT OR HIGH

LET ME BE EASY ON THE MAN THAT'S DOWN
LET ME BE SQUARE AND GENEROUS WITH ALL

I'M CARELESS SOMETIMES LORD WHEN I'M IN TOWN
BUT NEVER LET 'EM SAY I'M MEAN OR SMALL !

MAKE ME AS BIG AND OPEN AS THE PLAINS
AS HONEST AS THE HAWSE BETWEEN MY KNEES
CLEAN AS THE WIND THAT BLOWS BEHIND THE RAINS
FREE AS THE HAWK THAT CIRCLES DOWN THE BREEZE!

FORGIVE ME LORD IF SOMETIMES I FORGET
YOU KNOW ABOUT THE REASONS THAT ARE HID
YOU UNDERSTAND THE THINGS THAT GALL AND FRET
YOU KNOW ME BETTER THAN MY MOTHER DID

JUST KEEP AN EYE ON ALL THAT'S DONE AND SAID AND
RIGHT ME SOMETIMES WHEN I TURN ASIDE AND
GUIDE ME ON THE LONG DIM TRAIL AHEAD
THAT STRETCHES...TOWARD THE GREAT DIVIDE

BADGER CLARK   A COWBOY'S PRAYER

nothing much happened in Luckenbach this month
except
the potato chip man came by
I forgot that
and then there was daylight

a Luckenbach daylight
is that time of day you wish

would never go away··· when···

BANG!··· all of a sudden there's no dark and there's no light···
and it's foggy···
and it isn't

it's as

humble as life being born AIN'T THAT NEARLY A BLESSING
daylight on earth is when light is busy making little old nothings into something
and sometimes big brown bears turn into just big brown rocks

daylight in the wintertime
is when little dripping icicles get a new hold on their host
and jack frost is busy rolling up his carpet always from east to west
that covers the hills we love so

daylight in spring
is when little dew drops are just clingin' onto grass tips
just shiverin' from fright in the early morning light—
cause they know the sun is fixin' to love 'em to death
don't know why they shiver···it happens every morning!
I guess they have hope—

daylight in the summer
is when little ol' ladies are thinking about
puttin' on big ol' bonnets and long sleeves
                    to hide from the sun
and little young ladies are thinkin' about taking
off all their clothes to lie in it   SCARE ME !

and mama's thinking about pulling the shades in the living room
where NOBODY has really ever lived ...
                so the sun won't sadden the colors of the rug

daylight in the fall
is when big-eyed deer get closer to the ground
                        ...cause they know

red-eyed hunters with heavy rifles will soon be stumbling
                through the brush again

                        ..and again.. and again

and big trees brace themselves
the first norther's gonna tug pretty colors
                    out of just plain leaves
                    ...and then walk off

a Luckenbach daylight
is that magic time of day when there's just
thousands and thousands of insignificant miracles happening
      little quiet night feet are softly remembering their way home
      ...and soon their little delicate night tracks
      will be erased by big fuzzy day ones

and the squawkin' mockin'bird will wake the sun
      and the sun will tell the mama hoot owl it's time to fuss her big-eyed babies to bed
      and all the stars that were admired last night will take a back seat in the bus
      and the fantastic firefly will be just a bug
            but a giant weed will turn into a beautiful sunflower!
      then there's that unbelievable ...unbelievable smell of fresh coffee
      and leathery ranchers sittin' around sippin' too many cups
   just to keep from going to work
until the distant, instant naggin' of a chain saw jerks 'em back into reality

            little empty lunch pails are meetin' full ones on the freeway

you know...my music-makin' friends never get to enjoy all this
they're too busy racing the day home

                        sad folks wake up and say,
                           'NUTHER DAY

I wake up and say,

THERE SHE IS AGAIN !

THERE IT IS !

isn't that funny...
all this pretty stuff doesn't happen
unless I'm there

I get on my knees and
pat the earth and say,

GOD, YOU DONE IT AGAIN !

GOD, YOU DONE GOOD

THANK YOU, FELLER ···FRIEND

hondo crouch
1915-1976

I have no other helper than you

no other father, no other support
I pray to you
only you can help me

my present misery is too great

despair grips me

and I am at my wits' end
I am sunk in the depths
and I cannot pull myself up or out

if it is Your will
        help me out of this misery

let me know that You are stronger
            than all misery and
            all enemies
O Lord, if I come through this,
        please let the experience
        contribute to my
        and my brother's blessing

You will not forsake me
this I know amen

anonymous

at least to pray
is left
is left
O Jesus
in the air
I know not which
thy chamber is
I'm knocking
everywhere

emily dickinson
1880-1886

God made sun and moon to distinguish
seasons and day and night
and we cannot have the fruits of the earth
but in their seasons · but God hath made no decree to
distinguish the seasons of His mercies·
in paradise the
fruits were ripe the first minute · and in heaven it
is always autumn · His mercies
are ever in their maturity....

God never says
you should have come yesterday
He never says
you must come again tomorrow
but today
if you will hear His voice
today He will hear you....

He brought
    light out of darkness
    not out of lesser light
    He can bring thy
    summer out of winter
    though thou have no spring....

All occasions invite His Mercies
and all Times are His Seasons

John Donne
1573-1631

WILT THOU FORGIVE THAT SINNE WHERE I BEGUNNE,

WHICH WAS MY SINNE

        THOUGH IT WERE DONE BEFORE?

WILT THOU FORGIVE THAT SINNE

        THROUGH WHICH I RUNNE,

        AND DO RUNNE STILL,

    THOUGH STILL I DO DEPLORE?

    WHEN THOU HAST DONE,
    THOU HAST NOT DONE;

    FOR I HAVE MORE.

WILT THOU FORGIVE THAT SINNE

BY WHICH I HAVE WONNE OTHERS TO SINNE,

AND MADE MY SINNES THEIR DOORE?

WILT THOU FORGIVE THAT SINNE

WHICH I DID SHUNNE A YEARE OR TWO,

BUT WALLOWED IN, A SCORE?

WHEN THOU HAST DONE,
THOU HAST NOT DONE;

FOR I HAVE MORE.

I HAVE A SINNE OF FEARE,
THAT WHEN I HAVE SPUNNE MY LAST THREAD,
I SHALL PERISH
ON THE SHORE;
BUT
SWEARE BY THYSELFE
THAT AT MY DEATH
THY SONNE SHALL SHINE AS HE SHINES NOW,
AND HERETOFORE:

AND HAVING DONE THAT,
THOU HAST DONE;

I FEARE NO MORE.

JOHN DONNE

let not my mind be blinder

by more light

nor faith

by reason

added

lose

her sight

john donne

I.   And pray to God to have mercy upon us
And I pray that I may forget
Those matters that with myself I too much discuss
Too much explain
Because I do not hope to turn again
Let these words answer
For what is done, not to be done again
May the judgement not be too heavy upon us

Because these wings are no longer wings to fly
But merely vans to beat the air
The air which is now thoroughly small and dry
Smaller and dryer than the will
Teach us to care and not to care
Teach us to sit still

Pray for us sinners
now and at the hour of our death
Pray for us now and at the hour of our death

VI.   TEACH
US TO CARE
AND NOT TO CARE
TEACH
US TO SIT STILL
EVEN AMONG THESE ROCKS

OUR PEACE IN HIS WILL

AND EVEN AMONG THESE ROCKS

SISTER   MOTHER AND

SPIRIT OF THE RIVER

SPIRIT OF THE SEA

SUFFER ME NOT
TO BE SEPARATED

AND

LET MY CRY
COME UNTO THEE

T·S ELIOT
1888-1965

as I think of this Great Plan
I fall on my knees
         before the Father
            from whom all fatherhood
            earthly or heavenly
                    derives its name

and I pray that out of the glorious richness of
His resources He will enable you
to know the strength of the
Spirit's inner re-inforcement
that Christ may actually live
in your hearts by your faith

And I pray that you rooted and founded
in Love yourselves may be able to grasp
with all Christians

how wide and
long and deep and
high is the Love of Christ
and to know for yourselves
that love so far above our understanding
So will you be filled
through all your being with God Himself!
Now to Him who
by His power within us is
able to do infinitely more than
we ever dare to ask or imagine to Him be glory in the
Church and in Christ Jesus for ever and ever
amen!

St. Paul in
Ephesians 3:14-21

O Thou, who art the true
Sun of the world
ever rising, and
never going
down
Who by Thy most wholesome
appearing and sight
dost nourish and
gladden all things
in heaven
and
earth

we beseech Thee
   mercifully to shine into
our hearts, that
                   the night
             and darkness of sin
          and the mists of error
                   on every side
             being driven away
             by the brightness of
          Thy shining within our hearts
      we may all our life
walk without
          stumbling as in the
                        day-time
          and being pure and clean
                from the works of darkness
   may abound
         in all good works
      which Thou hast prepared
               for us to walk in
                        amen

                   erasmus   1467- 1536

OH····THIS PEOPLE
HAVE SINNED A
GREAT SIN···········
AND HAVE MADE
THEM GODS OF
GOLD·····YET NOW
·········IF THOU WILT
FORGIVE THEIR SIN

AND IF NOT·······
BLOT ME·········I
PRAY THEE···OUT
OF THY BOOK
WHICH THOU
HAST WRITTEN

MOSES IN EXODUS 32

Create in me a
CLEAN HEART

O God

and renew a
RIGHT SPIRIT

within me

cast me not away
from Thy presence

and take not Thy
Holy Spirit from me
restore unto me

King David responds in prayer after the Prophet Nathan confronts him with his sin in seducing Bathsheba and arranging the death of her husband

the joy of Thy SALVATION
and uphold
me with Thy FREE SPIRIT

David from Fifty·First Psalm

O LORD

BLESS MY WIFE

AND

MY SON JOHN

AND

HIS WIFE

US FOUR

AND

NO MORE

AMEN

FOLKPRAYER OF THE FRONTIER

FORGIVE

O LORD

MY

LITTLE JOKES

ON THEE

AND

I'LL
FORGIVE
THY GREAT BIG ONE
ON ME

ROBERT FROST
1874-1963

O Merciful God,
Be Thou unto me a strong
    tower of defence,
      I humbly entreat Thee.

Give me grace to await Thy leisure,
    and patiently to bear what Thou
    doest unto me;
      nothing doubting or mistrusting
      Thy goodness towards me;
      for Thou knowest what is good for
      me better than I do.

Therefore do with me in all things
       what Thou wilt;
       only arm me,
       I beseech Thee,
       with Thine armour,
       that I may stand fast;
       above all things, taking to me the
       shield of faith;
       praying always that I may refer
       myself wholly to Thy will,
       abiding Thy pleasure,
       and comforting myself in those
       troubles which it shall please Thee
       to send me,
       seeing such troubles are profitable
       for me;
       and I am assuredly persuaded that
       all Thou doest cannot but be well;
       and unto Thee be
       all Honour and Glory.
       Amen

Lady Jane Grey 1537-1554
          prayed during her last imprisonment

O Lord,
do not let William
grow up too quickly.
may he make no Decisions
without consulting me first.
may he still find his greatest Pleasure
in my company.

I know he is
developing new interests,
and making new friends,
but I do want to share in
every part of his Life.
remind him constantly of
all that he Owes to his parents.
Prevent him from
growing too independent.
and if he must have a Girl,
let it be that
sweet little Cynthia Black

prayer from a natural parent

David Head
1959

O Lord,
> in whose hands are life and death,
> by whose power I am sustained,
> and by whose mercy I am spared,
> ## look down upon me with pity.

Forgive me that I have
> until now so much
> ## neglected the duty
> which Thou hast assigned to me,
> and suffered the days and hours
> of which I must give account
> to pass away without any endeavor
> to accomplish Thy will.

Make me to remember, O God, that
> ## every day is Thy gift,
> and ought to be used according to
> Thy command.

Grant me, therefore,

so to repent of my negligence,
that I may obtain mercy from Thee, and
pass the time which Thou shalt yet allow me
in diligent performance of Thy commands,
through Jesus Christ. Amen

Samuel Johnson 1709-1784

all praise to thee, my God, this night
for all the blessings of the light;
keep me, o keep me, king of kings,
beneath Thine own almighty wings

forgive me, lord, for Thy dear Son,
the ill that 1 this day have done
that with the world, myself and Thee,
1, ere 1 sleep, at peace may be

teach me to live that 1 may dread
the grave as little as my bed;
teach me to die that so 1 may
rise glorious at the judgment day

o may my soul on Thee repose
and with sweet sleep mine eyelids close;
sleep that may me
more vigorous make
to serve my God
when I awake

praise God
from whom
all blessings
flow; praise Him
all creatures here below
praise Him above
ye heavenly host
praise Father
Son and

Holy Ghost

Bishop Thomas Ken
written about 1695

THE TUMULT AND
THE SHOUTING DIES
THE CAPTAINS AND
THE KINGS DEPART

STILL STANDS
THINE ANCIENT SACRIFICE

AN HUMBLE AND
A CONTRITE HEART

LORD GOD OF HOSTS
BE WITH US YET
LEST WE FORGET

LEST WE FORGET

RUDYARD KIPLING
FROM RECESSIONAL

We most earnestly beseech Thee
                    O Thou lover of mankind
                    to bless all Thy people
                    the flocks of Thy fold
Send down into our hearts
                    the peace of heaven and
            grant us also the peace of this life
Give life to the souls of all of us
        and let no deadly sin prevail against us
                    or any of Thy people
Deliver all who are in trouble
                    for Thou art our God
            Who settest the captives free
            Who givest hope to the hopeless
                    and help to the helpless
            Who liftest up the fallen and
Who art the Haven of the shipwrecked

Give Thy pity, pardon and
               refreshment to every Christian soul
                    whether in affliction or error
Preserve us in our pilgrimage
          through this life from hurt and danger
And grant that we may end our lives
               as Christians, well-pleasing to Thee
                    and free from sin
                    and that we may have
                    our portion and lot
                    with all Thy saints
 for the sake of Jesus Christ
 our Lord and Saviour
                    Amen

                              Liturgy of
                                   St. Mark
                              AD 175

when the father of an epileptic boy
         asks Jesus to cure him,

Jesus answers
        that all things are possible
               to those who believe,

                    the father responds:

LORD,

I  BELIEVE

HELP THOU

MINE

UNBELIEF

MARK 9:24

O God, Who art, and wast, and art to come,
    before Whose face the generations rise
    and pass away:
Age after age the living seek Thee and find
    that of Thy faithfulness there is no end.
Our fathers in their pilgrimage walked by
    Thy guidance, and rested on Thy compassion;
still to their
children
be Thou the Cloud by day
    and the Fire by night.

Where but in Thee have we
a covert from the storm,
    or shadow from
        the heat of life?
In our manifold temptations,
    Thou alone knowest
    and art ever nigh;

in sorrow, Thy pity revives the fainting soul;
        in our prosperity and ease,
    it is Thy spirit only that can keep us
        from pride and keep us humble.

O Thou sole source of
Peace and Righteousness,
take now the veil from every heart,
and join us in one communion
with Thy prophets and saints,
who have trusted in Thee
and were not ashamed.
Not of our worthiness, but of **Thy Tender Mercy,**

hear our prayer;
for the sake of
Jesus Christ,
Thy Son, our Lord
— Amen

James Martineau
1805-1900

The Lord's Prayer

OUR FATHER
WHICH ART IN HEAVEN
HALLOWED BE
THY NAME

THY KINGDOM COME
THY WILL BE DONE
IN EARTH AS IT
IS IN HEAVEN

GIVE US THIS DAY OUR DAILY BREAD

AND
FORGIVE US OUR DEBTS
AS WE FORGIVE OUR DEBTORS

AND
LEAD US NOT INTO TEMPTATION
BUT DELIVER US FROM EVIL

FOR THINE IS THE KINGDOM AND
THE POWER AND
THE GLORY
FOR EVER

AMEN

MATTHEW 6:9-13

Jesus in Gethsemane prays:

O My Father
if it be possible
let this cup
pass from me

nevertheless

    not as I will

  but as Thou wilt

              Matthew 26:39

O LORD

SUPPORT US ALL THE DAY LONG

UNTIL THE EVENING COMES AND

THE BUSY WORLD IS HUSHED AND

THE FEVER OF LIFE IS OVER AND

OUR WORK IS DONE

THEN IN THY MERCY

GRANT US A SAFE LODGING AND

A HOLY REST AND

PEACE AT THE LAST

THROUGH JESUS CHRIST OUR LORD
AMEN

JOHN HENRY, CARDINAL NEWMAN
1801-1890

Lord Thou knowest better than I know myself that I am growing older and will someday be old

Keep me from the fatal habit of thinking
I must say something
on every subject and on every occasion
Release me from craving to straighten out
everybody's affairs
Make me thoughtful but not moody
—·— helpful but not bossy
With my vast store of wisdom —·— it seems a pity not
to use it all.   But Thou knowest Lord that
I want a few friends at the end

Keep my mind free from the recital
of endless details Give me wings to get to the point
Seal my lips on my aches and pains. They are increasing
—·— and love of rehearsing them is becoming
sweeter as the time goes by
I dare not ask for grace enough to enjoy the tales of
other's pains —·— but help me to endure
them with patience—

I dare not ask for improved memory But for
a growing humility and a lessening cocksureness
when my memory seems to clash with the
memories of others
Teach me the glorious lesson that
occasionally I may be mistaken

Keep me reasonably sweet I do not want to be a saint
~·~ some of them are so hard to live with
But a sour old person is one of the crowning works of
the devil

Give me the ability to see good things in
unexpected places and talents in unexpected people
And give me ~·~
O Lord ~·~ the Grace to tell them so

a seventeenth century Nun

BLESS THE LORD
O MY SOUL
AND FORGET NOT ALL HIS BENEFITS

WHO FORGIVETH ALL THINE INIQUITIES
WHO HEALETH ALL THY DISEASES
WHO REDEEMETH THY LIFE FROM DESTRUCTION
WHO CROWNETH THEE WITH LOVING-KINDNESS
AND TENDER MERCIES
WHO SATISFIETH THY MOUTH WITH GOOD THINGS

SO THAT THY YOUTH IS RENEWED
LIKE THE EAGLE'S....

THE LORD IS MERCIFUL
AND GRACIOUS
SLOW TO ANGER
AND PLENTEOUS IN MERCY

HE WILL NOT ALWAYS CHIDE
NEITHER WILL HE KEEP HIS ANGER FOR EVER

HE HATH NOT DEALT WITH US AFTER OUR SINS
NOR REWARDED US ACCORDING TO OUR INIQUITIES

FOR AS THE HEAVEN
IS HIGH ABOVE THE EARTH
   SO GREAT IS HIS MERCY
   TOWARD THEM THAT FEAR HIM....

      AS FAR AS THE EAST
      IS FROM THE WEST
         SO FAR HATH HE REMOVED
         OUR TRANSGRESSIONS FROM US

         LIKE AS A FATHER

         PITIETH HIS CHILDREN

         SO THE LORD PITIETH THEM

         THAT FEAR HIM

DAVID IN THE
ONE HUNDRED·THIRD PSALM

O LORD thou hast searched me
and known me

thou knowest my downsitting and mine uprising
thou understandest my thought afar off
thou compassest my path and my lying down
and art acquainted with all my ways

for there is not a word in my tongue
                                    but lo: o lord *
            thou knowest it altogether
thou hast beset me behind and before
and laid thine hand upon me

such knowledge is too wonderful for me
it is high   I cannot attain unto it

SEARCH ME AND LEAD ME AND SEARCH

whither shall I go from thy spirit
or whither shall I flee from thy presence?
If I ascend up into heaven.. thou art there
If I make my bed in hell:: behold thou art there
If I take the wings of the morning
and dwell in the uttermost parts of the sea
even there shall thy hand lead me
and thy right hand shall hold me

If I say.: surely the darkness shall cover me
even the night shall be light about me
yea the darkness hideth not from thee
but the night shineth as the day
the darkness and the light are both alike to thee....
how precious also are thy thoughts unto me.:o god.:
how great is the sum of them!
If I should count them.: they are more in number
than the sand
when I awake
I am still with thee....

SEARCH ME
.:o god.:and know
my heart.:
try me
.:and know
my thoughts.:
and see if there
be any wicked
way in me.:
AND LEAD ME
in the
way everlasting

David in the
One Hundred Thirty.Ninth Psalm

Almighty God unto Whom
all hearts are open
all desires known
and from Whom
no secrets are hid
cleanse the thoughts of
our hearts
by the inspiration of Thy
Holy Spirit
that we may
perfectly Love Thee
and worthily magnify
Thy Holy Name
through Christ
our Lord
Amen

The Book of Common Prayer

Defend
O Lord
this Thy child
with Thy heavenly grace
That he may continue
Thine for ever
And daily increase in
Thy Holy Spirit
more and more
Until he come unto
Thy everlasting
kingdom
Amen

from The Order of Confirmation

The Book of Common Prayer

ALMIGHTY AND MOST MERCIFUL FATHER

WE HAVE ERRED AND STRAYED
FROM THY WAYS
LIKE LOST SHEEP

WE HAVE FOLLOWED TOO MUCH THE
DEVICES AND DESIRES OF OUR OWN HEARTS

WE HAVE OFFENDED AGAINST THY
HOLY LAWS

WE HAVE LEFT UNDONE THOSE THINGS WHICH WE
OUGHT TO HAVE DONE AND

WE HAVE DONE
THOSE THINGS WHICH WE
OUGHT NOT
TO HAVE DONE
AND
THERE IS NO
HEALTH IN US

BUT THOU, O LORD,
HAVE MERCY UPON US
MISERABLE OFFENDERS

SPARE THOU THOSE O GOD
WHO CONFESS THEIR FAULTS

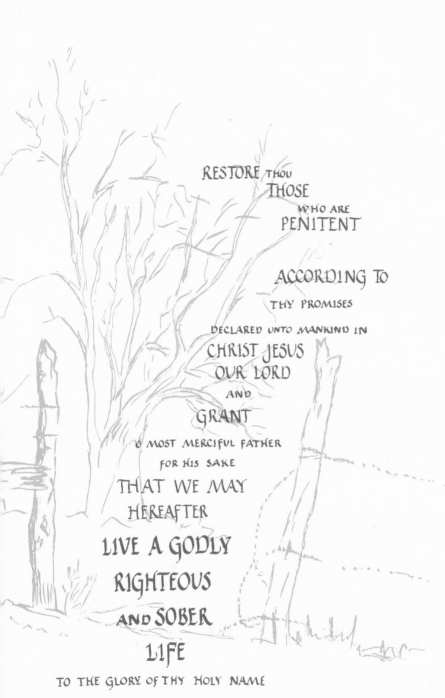

RESTORE THOU
THOSE
WHO ARE
PENITENT

ACCORDING TO
THY PROMISES
DECLARED UNTO MANKIND IN
CHRIST JESUS
OUR LORD
AND
GRANT
O MOST MERCIFUL FATHER
FOR HIS SAKE
THAT WE MAY
HEREAFTER
LIVE A GODLY
RIGHTEOUS
AND SOBER
LIFE
TO THE GLORY OF THY HOLY NAME
AMEN

THE BOOK OF COMMON PRAYER

Lord Jesus Eternal Priest

You have called me to
Your priesthood to carry on
the work which You began

Fit me, I pray You, for this task, with
such faith that through my voice even
the disbelieving may
listen to Your word
with such hope that
through my hands even
the despairing may
be held fast in Your grip

and with such
charity that through
my heart even
the despised may know that
You can never cease to Love them

join me so deeply
to Yourself that no one

an unknown
priest

I meet shall lie beyond
Your saving reach

O God,
        how poor I am
        how rich if I could
        still have prayer

O God,
        how low I am
        my mortal flight
        is on one floor

but I am tired of sitting on
        these chairs, homesick
        for that upper room

it makes me think of
    those old altar stairs
    and wonder
    if they would still
    hold my weight

there was a door up there
    he used to keep unlocked
    the latch was low
    and 1 could always open it
    IF 1 GOT DOWN
    UPON MY KNEES

david redding
1965

O heavenly Father

protect and bless

all things that have breath

guard them from all evil and

let them sleep in peace

Albert Schweitzer
1875 - 1965

O, my offence is rank, it smells to heaven;

it hath the primal eldest curse upon't,

a brother's murder.

Pray can I not,

though inclination be as sharp as will:

my stronger guilt defeats my strong intent,

and like a man to double business bound,

I stand in pause where I shall first begin,

and both neglect.

What if this cursed hand were thicker than itself with brother's blood,

is there not rain enough in the sweet heavens to wash it white as snow?

Whereto serves mercy but to confront the visage of offense?

And what's in prayer but this twofold force,

to be forestalled ere we come to fall,

or pardon'd being down?

Then I'll look up;

my fault is past.

But, O, what form of prayer can serve my turn?

"Forgive me my foul murder?"

That cannot be,

since I am still possess'd of those effects for which I did the murder;

my crown,

mine own ambition

and my queen.

May one be pardon'd and retain the offense?
In the corrupted currents of this world
offense's gilded hand may shove by justice,
and oft 'tis seen the wicked prize itself buys out the law:
but 'tis not so above:
there is no shuffling,
there the action lies in his true nature,
and we ourselves compell'd
even to the teeth and forehead of our faults
to give in evidence.
What then?
What rests?
Try what repentance can:
what can it not?
Yet what can it when one can not repent?
O wretched state!
O bosom black as death!
O limed soul,
that struggling to be free art more engaged!
Help, angels!
Make assay!
Bow,
stubborn knees, and,
heart with strings of steel,
be soft as sinews of the new-born babe!

All may be well....
My words fly up, my thoughts remain below:
Words without thoughts never to heaven go

william shakespeare: hamlet
act III, scene III
spoken by usurping king Claudius who murdered Hamlet's father

depart from me

for I am a
sinful man,
O Lord

Simon Peter

in Luke 5:8

O Lord,
  I ain't what I wanna be

O Lord,
  I ain't what I oughta be

and
O Lord,
  I ain't what I'm gonna be

but thanks, Lord,
  I ain't what I used to be

Prayer of a Long-Dead Slave

then Solomon stood before the altar of the Lord
in the presence of all the assembly of Israel and
spread forth his hands
toward heaven and said   O LORD, God of Israel

there is no God like Thee

in heaven above or on earth beneath....

now therefore

O God of Israel

let Thy word be confirmed

which Thou hast spoken

to Thy servant David my father

but will God indeed
dwell on the earth?
behold
heaven and the
highest
heaven
cannot
contain
Thee

how
much
less this
house
which
I have
built !

yet have regard
to the prayer of Thy servant and to his supplication
O Lord my God

hearkening to the cry and to the prayer which Thy servant prays before Thee this day

that Thy eyes may be open night and day toward this house

the place of which Thou hast said My name shall be there....

and hearken Thou to the supplication of Thy servant and of Thy people Israel
when they pray toward this place
yea, hear Thou in heaven Thy dwelling place

and when Thou hearest, forgive....

if there is famine in the land

if there is pestilence or
blight or
mildew or
locust or
caterpillar

if their enemy besieges them in any of their cities

whatever plague
whatever sickness there is
whatever prayer
whatever supplication is made by any man
or by all Thy people Israel
each knowing the affliction of his own heart and
stretching out his hands toward this house

then HEAR Thou in heaven Thy dwelling place and
FORGIVE and
ACT and
RENDER to each whose heart Thou knowest
according to all his ways
for Thou
Thou only
knowest the hearts
of all the children of men
that they may fear Thee
all the days that they live in the land
which Thou gavest to our fathers

Solomon
in I Kings 8:22-40

HOW SIMPLE FOR ME TO LIVE
HOW EASY TO BELIEVE

when in confusion my soul bares itself or bends

when the most wise can see no

WITH YOU, OH LORD
IN YOU

further than this night and do not know what the morrow brings

You fill me with the clear certainty that

You exist and that You watch to see that all

the paths of righteousness be not closed

from the heights of wordly glory

I am astonished by

the path through despair

You have provided me

this path from

which I have been worthy enough

to reflect Your radiance to man

all that I will yet reflect, You will grant me

and

for that which I will not succeed in reflecting

You have appointed others

alexander solzhenitsyn
1962

Lord, I give up all my own plans
and purposes
all my own desires
and hopes
and accept Thy will
for my life

I give

betty scott stam

myself
my life
my all
utterly to Thee
to be Thine forever
fill me and seal me with
Thy Holy Spirit
use me as Thou wilt
send me where Thou wilt
work out Thy whole will
in my life at any cost
now and forever

Lord, behold our family here assembled

We thank Thee
for this place in which we dwell

for the Love that unites us

for the peace accorded us this day

for the Hope with which
we expect the morrow

for the health
the work
the food and
the bright skies
that make our
Lives Delightful

for our Friends
in all parts
of the earth ....

Give us Courage and Gaiety and the Quiet Mind....

Bless us
if it may be
in all our innocent endeavors
    if it may not
give us the strength to encounter
that which is to come

    that we may be
    Brave in peril
    Constant in tribulation
    Temperate in wrath

        and in all changes of fortune
        and down to the gates of death
        Loyal and Loving one to another

        As the clay to the potter
        as the windmill to the wind
        as children of their sire

            We beseech of Thee
            this Help and Mercy
            for Christ's sake

robert louis stevenson
    1850-1894

DEAREST LORD
MAY I SEE YOU TODAY
AND EVERY DAY
IN THE PERSON OF YOUR SICK
AND
WHILST NURSING THEM
MINISTER UNTO YOU

THOUGH YOU HIDE YOURSELF
BEHIND THE UNATTRACTIVE DISGUISE
OF THE IRRITABLE
THE EXACTING
THE UNREASONABLE
MAY I STILL RECOGNIZE YOU AND SAY
"Jesus, my patient, how sweet it is to serve you"

LORD, GIVE ME THIS SEEING FAITH
THEN MY WORK WILL NEVER BE MONOTONOUS
I WILL EVER FIND JOY IN HUMOURING THE FANCIES AND
GRATIFYING THE WISHES
OF ALL POOR SUFFERERS

O BELOVED SICK
HOW DOUBLY DEAR
YOU ARE TO ME
WHEN YOU PERSONIFY CHRIST
AND
WHAT A PRIVILEGE IS MINE
TO BE ALLOWED TO TEND YOU

SWEETEST LORD, MAKE ME APPRECIATIVE OF THE DIGNITY
OF MY HIGH VOCATION · AND ITS MANY RESPONSIBILITIES

NEVER PERMIT ME
TO DISGRACE IT
BY GIVING WAY
TO COLDNESS
UNKINDNESS OR
IMPATIENCE

AND O GOD,
WHILE YOU ARE JESUS
MY PATIENT
DEIGN ALSO TO BE
TO ME A PATIENT JESUS
BEARING WITH MY FAULTS
LOOKING ONLY TO MY INTENTION
which is
TO LOVE and SERVE YOU
IN THE PERSON OF
EACH OF YOUR SICK

LORD · INCREASE MY FAITH
BLESS MY EFFORTS
AND WORK
NOW AND FOR
EVERMORE   AMEN

mother Teresa

the Lord is my shepherd

I shall not want
He maketh me to lie down in green pastures
He leadeth me beside the still waters
He restoreth my soul
He leadeth me in the paths of righteousness
for His name's sake

Yea, though I walk through the valley
of the shadow of death
I will fear no evil
For Thou art with me
Thy rod and Thy staff
they comfort me

Thou
preparest
a table before me
in the presence of mine enemies
Thou anointest my head with oil
My cup runneth over

Surely goodness and
mercy shall follow me all the days of my life

and I

will dwell
in the house
of the Lord
for ever

david in the Twenty-third psalm

the dying words of
William Tyndale who was
burned at the stake
by order of King Henry VIII
for translating
the Bible into English

Lord, open the King of England's eyes

William Tyndale
1494-1536

ALMIGHTY GOD
WHO HAST GIVEN US
THIS GOOD LAND FOR OUR HERITAGE
we humbly beseech Thee
that we may always prove ourselves a people
mindful of Thy favor and glad to do Thy will

BLESS OUR LAND with honorable industry
·sound learning· and pure manners

SAVE US from·violence ·discord· and confusion ···
from pride and arrogancy ~~~and from every evil way

DEFEND OUR LIBERTIES
and fashion into one happy people the multitudes
brought hither out of many kindreds and tongues

Endue with the spirit of wisdom
those to whom in Thy name
we entrust
the authority of government
·that there may be justice and peace
at home ~ and that· through obedience t

Thy law · we may show

forth Thy praise among the nations of the earth

IN THE TIME OF PROSPERITY

FILL OUR HEARTS WITH THANKFULNESS and

IN THE DAY OF TROUBLE

SUFFER NOT OUR TRUST IN THEE TO FAIL

all which we ask through
Jesus Christ
our Lord
Amen

The Book of Common Worship

now unto him
that is able to do
exceeding abundantly
above all that
we ask or think
according to the power
that worketh in us

unto him be glory
in the church
by christ jesus
throughout all ages
world without end
amen

the book of common worship

O God from Whom cometh every good
and perfect gift

grant unto all young
men and women
that they may be
worthy of their
heritage

Quicken their minds in the desire for knowledge and
their hearts in the love of virtue—
Deliver them from fear of that which is new and
from scorn of that which is old
Lead them forward in the spirit of understanding and
Confirm them in the confidence that all truth is
for their good and to Thy glory

Out of weakness give them strength
support them in the time of temptation
help them to do Thy work with good courage and
Continue Thy faithful soldiers and servants
until their life's end
Through Jesus Christ our Lord
amen

the book of common worship

the Lord
    bless you and
    keep you

the Lord
    make His face to shine
        upon you and
    be gracious unto you

the Lord
    lift up
        His countenance
        upon you and

                give you peace

through
Jesus
Christ
our Lord

amen

book of common Worship

contents and acknowledgments
listed in order of appearance

Sören Kierkegaard (1813 - 1855), Danish writer and philosopher; © 1940 by Augsburg Publishing House, Minneapolis; taken from **For Self-Examination** — Recommended for the times by S. Kierkegaard, translated from the Danish by Edna and Howard Hong; used by permission.

St. Francis of Assisi (1182 - 1226), Italian monk and preacher; "This prayer is popularly attributed to St. Francis, but some references list it under 'Anonymous'."

Baron Jacob Astley (1579 - 1652), royalist commander in English Civil War; found in reference works of familiar quotations.

St. Augustine (354 - 430 AD), Bishop of Hippo, North Africa; adapted and taken from his **Confessions**; two entries. Taken from **Masterpieces of Religious Verse,** edited by James Dalton Morrison (New York, Harper & Row, publishers).

Thomas Blake, Attributed; "I've loved this old and beautiful prayer for many years and have it attributed to Thomas Blake in my notes, although some sources say it is an anonymous work."

Author Unknown; "This great familiar prayer, sometimes called 'The Serenity Prayer,' is reprinted extensively in the literature of Alcoholics Anonymous. They list it under 'Anonymous' and other sources attribute it to the theologian Reinhold Niebuhr. In my notes, however, I have written that it comes from Pastor Friedrich Christoph and was written in 1782. I believe this is correct."

Booger Boles; © 1977 by The Zondervan Corporation; quoted by David A. Redding from his book **Jesus Makes Me Laugh** (Grand Rapids, Zondervan Publishing House, 1977); used by permission; "Booger was a blond long-hair young man in my congregation back when long hair on men was an offense to most adults. He spoke this prayer spontaneously when he was my assistant one Sunday and one of my older parishioners described it later as an act of communion."

Robert Burns (1759 - 1796), Scottish national poet; titled "Prayer in the Prospect of Death," taken from **Poems and Songs of Robert Burns,** edited by James Barke (London, Collins, 1953).

A Child's Prayer, traditional.

The Rev. Dr. John R. Claypool *(1970), minister of Northminster Baptist Church, Jackson, Mississippi; used by permission of the author and published here for the first time.*

The Concord Anthem Book *(Concord Series No. 13);* © *1925 by E.C. Schirmer Music Company, Boston; taken from Psalm 5:8; 4:8; used with permission.*

Prayer of an Unknown Confederate Soldier; *taken from* **A Third Treasury of the Familiar,** *edited by Ralph L. Woods (New York, Macmillan Publishing Co., Inc., 1970).*

A Cowboy's Prayer *(Written for Mother, by Badger Clark (d. 1957);* © *1922 by The Westerners Foundation; taken from* **Sun and Saddle Leather,** *a book of Badger Clark's poems, published by The Westerners Foundation, Badger Clark Memorial Center, Dakota Wesleyan University, Mitchell, S.D.*

Hondo Crouch *(1915 - 1976); titled "Luckenbach Daylight" by John Russell (Hondo) Crouch,* © *1978 by Grape Creek Music, BMI, San Antonio, Texas; used by permission; "Hondo was a friend of mine, a goat rancher and promoter who once bought the town of Luckenbach. He was sometimes called 'the Clown Prince of Texas' and folks knew him as a kind of Will Rogers character. His daughter, Becky Patterson, sent me a copy of this prayer and it is being published for the first time in this book. Becky's husband, Dow, is President of Grape Creek Music, BMI."*

Anonymous; *taken from* **I Lie On My Mat And Pray,** *edited by Fritz Pawelzik (New York, Friendship Press, 1964), used by permission.*

Emily Dickinson *(1830 - 1886); first verse of J. 502 taken from* **The Complete Poems of Emily Dickinson,** *edited by Thomas H. Johnson (Boston, Little, Brown and Company).*

John Donne *(1573 - 1631), English metaphysical poet and cleric; the work which begins "Wilt thou forgive that sinne. . . ." is titled: "A Hymne to God the Father" taken from* **The Complete Poetry and Selected Prose of John Donne,** *edited by Charles Coffin (New York, Random House, Inc. 1952); the other selections are untitled and found in reference works of familiar quotations; three entries.*

T. S. Eliot *(1888 - 1965); selected from Section I and Section IV of "Ash-Wednesday," 1930; taken from* **Collected Poems 1909 - 1935** *by T.S. Eliot (London, Faber & Faber Limited, 1936).*

St. Paul *in Ephesians 3:14-21; taken from "The Letter to the Christians at Ephesus,"* **The New Testament in Modern English,** *Revised Edition, translated by J.B. Phillips;* © *by J.B. Phillips 1958, 1960, 1972 (New York, Macmillan Publishing Co., Inc.); used by permission.*

Erasmus *(1467 - 1536), Dutch philosopher; taken from* **The Meaning of Prayer,** *by Harry Emerson Fosdick (New York, Association Press, 1916).*

Moses *in Exodus 32; King James Version of the Bible.*

David *from Fifty-First Psalm; King James Version of the Bible.*

Folkprayer of the Frontier; *"Every farmer in the midwest knows this prayer as coming from a great grandparent."*

Robert Frost *(1874 - 1963);* © *1969 by Holt, Rinehart & Winston; taken from* **The Poetry of Robert Frost,** *edited by Edward Connery Lathem (New York, Holt, Rinehart & Winston, 1969); used by permission.*

Lady Jane Grey *(1537 - 1554); English noblewoman beheaded at age 17 as a possible rival for the throne; taken from* **The Meaning of Prayer** *by Harry Emerson Fosdick.*

David Head *(1962); titled "A Natural Parent";* © *1959 by The Epworth Press; taken from* **He Sent Leanness** — *A Book of Prayers for the Natural Man by David Head (New York, The Macmillan Company, 1962); used by permission.*

Herbie; © *1966 by Eric Marshall and Stuart Hample; taken from* **Children's Letters to God** *compiled by Marshall and Hample (New York, Simon & Schuster, 1966); used by permission.*

Samuel Johnson *(1709 - 1784), English author and lexicographer; taken from* **The Meaning of Prayer** *by Harry Emerson Fosdick.*

Bishop Thomas Ken *(1637 - 1711), English prelate and hymn writer; titled "Evening," taken from* **The Hymnal** *published by authority of The General Assembly of the Presbyterian Church in the United States of America, 1933 (Philadelphia).*

Rudyard Kipling *(1865 - 1936), English author and adventurer; second verse from "Recessional" written in 1897; taken from* **Rudyard Kipling's Verse** — *Definitive Edition (New York, Doubleday and Company, Inc., 1940).*

Liturgy of St. Mark *175 AD; titled "Intercession," taken from* **A Chain of Prayer Across the Ages** — *Forty Centuries of Prayer, from 2000 B.C. compiled by S.F. Fox (New York, E.P. Dutton and Company, Inc., 1943).*

Mark *9:24; King James Version of the Bible.*

James Martineau *(1805 - 1900), English theologian and philosopher; taken from* **The Book of Common Worship** *approved by the General Assembly of the Presbyterian Church in the United States of America (Philadelphia, 1946); used by permission.*

Matthew *6; King James Version of the Bible.*

Matthew *26:39; King James Version of the Bible.*

John Henry, Cardinal Newman *(1801 - 1890), English cleric and writer; taken from The Book of Common Worship; used by permission.*

Seventeenth Century Nun; *taken from a print without a listed source which was purchased in a London bookstore.*

David *in the One Hundred Third Psalm; King James Version of the Bible.*

David *in the One Hundred Thirty-Ninth Psalm; King James Version of the Bible.*

The Book of Common Prayer *and Administration of the Sacraments and Other Rites and Ceremonies of the Church according to the use of the Protestant Episcopal Church in the United States of America (New York, 1945).*

An Unknown Priest; *taken from a plaque.*

David A. Redding; © 1975 by David A. Redding; titled "At the Beginning," taken from his book *If I Could Pray Again* (Millbrae, California, Celestial Arts, 1975); used by permission.

Albert Schweitzer (1875 - 1965), French Protestant philosopher, theologian, musician, medical doctor in Africa; found in reference works of familiar quotations.

William Shakespeare (1564 - 1616), English dramatist and poet; taken from **Hamlet** by William Shakespeare (Chicago, The Great Books Foundation, 1966).

Simon Peter in Luke 5:8; King James Version of the Bible.

Prayer of a Long-Dead Slave; quoted by Gert Behanna in her book **God Is Not Dead** (Richmond, Texas, Well-Spring Center, 1977), with appreciation to Dr. Bardwell L. Smith and to Mrs. Joseph C. Wessendorff.

Solomon in I Kings 8:22-40; Revised Standard Version of the Bible.

Alexander Solzhenitsyn (1918 -), Russian novelist; © 1971 by Condé Nast Publications, Inc., taken from **Vogue** Magazine, Christmas issue 1971; used by permission; "Solzhenitsyn said this prayer was circulated in Russia in secret before it was published in this country. Here he expresses his deeply religious vision of man's future." Used by permission of the author.

Betty Scott Stam (d. 1934), martyred Christian missionary; quoted by Elisabeth Elliot in her book **Let Me Be a Woman** (Wheaton, Illinois, Tyndale House Publishers, Inc., 1976); used by permission.

Robert Louis Stevenson (1850 - 1894), Scottish author and poet; titled "For Success" from Vailima Prayers, taken from **The Life of Robert Louis Stevenson** by Graham Balfour, Vol. II (New York, Charles Scribner's Sons, 1901).

Mother Teresa (1910 -), Roman Catholic medical missionary in India; titled "Jesus My Patient," taken from **Something Beautiful for God** — Mother Teresa of Calcutta, by Malcolm Muggeridge (New York, Harper & Row, Publishers, 1971); used by permission.

David in the Twenty-Third Psalm; King James Version of the Bible.

William Tyndale (1494 - 1536), English reformer and martyr; quoted in **What Is the Man?** by David A. Redding (Waco, Texas, Word Books, 1970); used by permission. Taken from **The Work of William Tyndale,** edited by S.L. Greenslade (London & Glasgow, Blackie and Sons Ltd., 1938).

The Book of Common Worship approved by the General Assembly of the Presbyterian Church in the United States of America (Philadelphia, 1946); used by permission; four entries.

david a. redding

minister, nationally known speaker

and author of many inspirational books, including

LIVES HE TOUCHED   THE MIRACLES OF CHRIST
THE PARABLES HE TOLD   IF I COULD PRAY AGAIN
JESUS MAKES ME LAUGH

alice blue girand

*one of the nation's leading
calligraphers & author
of texts on lettering.
She uses her artistic &
design abilities in
teaching seminars &
in calligraphic
lettering*

sarah shortle blue

*Southwestern artist who
has shown her work
in galleries & juried shows.
She also illustrates
greeting cards for
use with calligraphy.*